BookLife
freedom
Readers

MY PET
GUINEA PIG

BY WILLIAM ANTHONY

BookLife
PUBLISHING

©2022
BookLife Publishing Ltd.
King's Lynn
Norfolk PE30 4LS

A catalogue record for this book is available from the British Library.

ISBN: 978-1-80155-137-3

Written by:
William Anthony

Edited by:
Madeline Tyler

Designed by:
Jasmine Pointer

Photocredits:

Images are courtesy of Shutterstock.com. With thanks to Getty Images, Thinkstock Photo and iStockphoto.

Front cover - Tatyana Vyc, Winning7799. 2 - StineMah. 3 - Vasily Kovalev, Africa Studio. 4 - In Green. 5 - Tatyana Vyc. 6 - Daisy Daisy. 7 - Tatyana Vyc. 8 - Dantyya. 9 - CatJB. 10 - JohnatAPW, Tim Large. 11 - Heder Zambrano. 12 - Fangfy. 13 - yurilily. 14 & 15 - Shchus. 16 - Monkey Business Images. 17 - Pressmaster. 18 - Chertamchu. 19 - DmitryPron. 20 - Dev_Maryna. 21 - Eric Isselee. 22 - Tatyana Vyc. 23 - Djem.

BookLife
freedom
Readers

CONTENTS

Zoe ♥ and Fudge

Hello! My name is Zoe, and this is my pet guinea pig, Fudge. He is four years old. He has a friend called Sherbet. They live together because guinea pigs like living in pairs.

Zoe

Fudge

I think Sherbet is sleeping at the moment, so it looks like it will just be me and Fudge. We will be talking you through how to look after guinea pigs.

Getting Guinea Pigs

Looking after guinea pigs means you are going to have a lot of responsibility. You will need to feed them and give them a nice home with lots of space.

My family got Fudge and Sherbet from a pet shop, but you can also get guinea pigs from a rescue centre or from a breeder. A breeder is someone who keeps guinea pigs to mate them. It is best to keep guinea pigs in pairs, so be ready to look after two animals.

Home

Guinea pigs do not like lots of loud noises. It can be quite noisy in a house, so it might be a good idea to keep them outside. If you keep them outside, make sure their home is warm and out of the wind.

They will need a cage with lots of space for exercise and a good shelter where they can sleep. You could get them tunnels for their cage to keep them entertained.

Playtime

Guinea pig run

Most guinea pigs have fun exploring. You could also get them a run so they can explore safely in your garden.

When you are playing with your guinea pigs, you must be very calm and gentle. Guinea pigs do not like loud noises so do not shout when you are petting them.

Food

Guinea pigs need food to stay alive, just like us. They are easy animals to feed. Guinea pigs need lots of hay and some pellet food, which you can get from any pet shop.

Pellet food

Guinea pigs need different types of food in their diet. You can also give your guinea pigs different types of vegetables. They like carrots, broccoli and cabbage. This keeps their diets healthy and balanced.

Bedtime

Sherbet is still sleeping. Shall we take a quick peek? He is sleeping on a soft and fluffy blanket. Guinea pigs also like to sleep on soft paper or wood shavings.

Sorry Sherbet, did we wake you? We will move on and let you get back to sleep! Guinea pigs usually have short naps, so he will be awake again soon.

The Vet

Guinea pigs can get ill, just like humans. Guinea pigs that are ill can go to the vets. Vets are like doctors, but for animals instead of humans. The vet will do everything they can to help your guinea pig get better again.

One day when I came home, Fudge was sneezing and had crusty eyes. I told my parents, and we took him to the vet, who made him all better again. If you think your guinea pig is not very well, make sure you tell an adult.

Growing Up

When guinea pigs get older, they find it hard to move as quickly as they used to. It is important to be gentle with older guinea pigs.

You could also try to make their cage more comfortable. Make sure they can reach their water easily and have somewhere soft to rest and sleep. You could even bring your elderly guinea pigs indoors to help them stay warm.

Super Guinea Pigs

All guinea pigs are amazing, but some guinea pigs are simply super. A guinea pig called Truffles holds the world record for the farthest jump by a guinea pig. He jumped 48 centimetres!

Another guinea pig, called Flash, holds the world record for the fastest 10-metre run. He ran it in just under nine seconds!

You ❤ and Your Pets

Whether you have young guinea pigs, old guinea pigs or super guinea pigs, make sure you take care of them just like Fudge and I have taught you.

I am sure you will make a great pet owner. I hope your new furry friends enjoy their new home, and that you have lots of fun together.

QUESTIONS ??

1: What do guinea pigs eat?

2: Name two places you can get a guinea pig from.

3: What do guinea pigs like to sleep on?
 a) Soft paper or wood shavings
 b) Pencils and pens
 c) Rocks and sticks

4: Name two things you could do for an old guinea pig.

5: Would you like a guinea pig? Why or why not?

BookLife
freedom
Readers